THE DOWNLOADING OF FILES INTO THE HUMAN PSYCHE

JOANNE TISDALE

Copyright © 2013 by Joanne Tisdale

The Downloading of Files into the Human Psyche
by Joanne Tisdale

Printed in the United States of America

ISBN 9781628711721

All rights reserved solely by the author. The author guarantees all contents are original and do not infringe upon the legal rights of any other person or work. No part of this book may be reproduced in any form without the permission of the author. The views expressed in this book are not necessarily those of the publisher.

Unless otherwise indicated, Bible quotations are taken from the King James Version. Copyright © 1990 by Thomas Nelson.

www.xulonpress.com

Contents

Acknowledgements vi
Forward ix
Introduction: The Many Faces of
the Human Computer xi

Chapter One	Comparative Behavior 13	
Chapter Two	Wrestling with Aloneness: When Is Self-Awareness Enough? 17	
Chapter Three	The Journey of Self-Discovery 19	
Chapter Four	A Storybook Life 27	
Chapter Five	Living Life in a Capsule 31	
Chapter Six	Word Power: Self-Evolving 37	
Chapter Seven	The Life of Domestication 43	
Chapter Eight	The Brain: The Files in the Human Computer 47	
Chapter Nine	Revisiting Past Downloads 51	
Chapter Ten	The Power of Affirmations on Downloaded Files 57	
Chapter Eleven	HodgePodge Ethics: Turning the Corner 59	
Chapter Twelve	Developing a File of Safe Thinking 63	
Chapter Thirteen	Thinking Outside "The Box" 65	
Chapter Fourteen	Integrative Thinking 69	
Chapter Fifteen	A Positive, Projected Future 71	
Chapter Sixteen	Conclusion 75	

Acknowledgements

*G*ratitude – my continued gratitude to my relentless editor, my sister, Gertie Mae Talton, a masterful, degreed English teacher. Thank you, Gertie. Agape' love to you.

This book is a culmination of the creations whose paths I have crossed, exclusively my family. My immediate family — George, Senior, Buffy, George, Junior, Stacey, and Nina. And to all readers who are visionary in their growth toward evolving, I graciously thank you. Love for all times, to you all. Thank "U"; thank "U".

Joanne

Forward

Why a book called, **THE DOWNLOADING OF FILES INTO THE HUMAN PSYCHE**? Some time ago, it came to my attention that the bulk of my life was being run by an incessant culmination of voluntary and involuntary mental downloading of files, which has been a conversation running rampant in my psyche. It occurred to me that others may be plagued with this unnamed virus as well.

I shared this book to stimulate your conscious and unconscious mind/life for the greater good of your journey here on the planet. Be blessed.

INTRODUCTION

The Many Faces of the Human Computer

*D*ownloading files has occurred for years, [yea], even decades and we wonder why people act as they do. It's archives — archives of unconsciously stuff being lived out of; we, the planet, being affected. That's where your mental, physical, spiritual, and all social ills evolve. Relationships disintegrate. We project! Presume! Assume! You begin to question your own purpose here on the planet and why you do what you do.

[As for myself], I've downloaded archives and archives — the art of not focusing is one of the downloads that I live out of. It is, therefore, an astronomical challenge to get the task done of deprogramming my own downloads. I'm not certain that, that was one of my coping mechanisms. You do know, that we download coping strategies into our lives as well, right?? They may be lethal, but we download a way to survive anyway. So, the conversations, the stories — all of that, that we will be looking at in this book is a derivative of a gazillion downloads.

CHAPTER ONE

Comparative Behavior

I have done extensive research on "thought life". My findings overwhelmingly conclude that everything originates from/with a thought. There is even a passage in the Bible that says, "As you think, so you behave." (**Proverbs 23:7**) All things being considered, everything originates with a thought.

Life is lovely when we choose not to make up stories in our head, even to the characters, the plot, and their positions which they all play. I am mindful at this point of my granddaughter's graduation. Because she and her dad, my son, live with me, I was anticipating her high school prom that was approaching. I concocted for myself an elaborate story of how it was going to play out – paparazzi and the works!! To my amazement, a different story was being played that did not include me or my residence. Anguish, coupled with weeks of discombobulating occurred that I made it up and HOW DARE I !! — act so controlling of another person's existence!! The beginning of my awareness. I created untold anguish – anguish for myself and possibly some cells died in my body as well – all because I did not live in the moment. Not being present can cause one to become grief-stricken.

The stories we tell ourselves about ourselves that we're not good enough, that you need another human being to define you, to cause you to see value in your intrinsic, innate magnificence.

Just talked to a 4th grader who is going to a different school next year. I said to the young lady: "If you come back to our school, please come by and say "Hello." And she remarked, "What if I don't want to?" I said to her, "That's okay." That's okay because I never allow other's behaviour to define me. Then I moved on. It's kind of like a journey here.

Again, I was talking to a group of 3rd graders and their teacher, and the teacher says, "They are a result of their home life." And I made a statement and this young man responded. I said, "You've touched me and I have grown." Just to see if he got what I was saying, I said to him, "Does it mean that (I reached out and touched his shoulder) – does it mean that because you touched with me with your hand or I touched you with my hand, that I am now growing, getting taller?" He said, "No, no! It means that you've learned something from me and you are becoming a better person for it." And I thought, "WOW!" And, of course, his teacher is standing there and she said, "Yeah! But they don't do what they know. They don't do what they know!" I said to her, "It is a process. It doesn't mean that you are not doing a great job; it's just a process of evolving." Then I asked her, "What about your [own] children? The first time you taught them something, did they get it or did it take some years of growing, some years of processing your teaching?" And she moved around in the conversation as to where she was not answering that. "WOW!"

Chapter Two

Wrestling with Aloneness: When Is Self-Awareness Enough?

As I was sitting in the school gym waiting for dismissal on Friday, June 1st, I found myself struggling to feel that sitting (just me) is alright. I am enough. That takes some really, really openness, some really self-defining to know that I have always had the power to feel sufficient. Just me and my great Creator. WOW!!

If I am believing that for decades, massive masses of people have misunderstood that we're never alone. I have concluded after enormous research—"I'm never alone; I cannot be alone!" The Energy, the Creator that created me, as I navigate on this planet, when I move, He that created me moves as well. That is so comforting and whenever I come up with a story that I am alone, it only means it is just a story – just a story.

The Downloading of Files into the Human Psyche

I think about a great friend of mine and she is so lovely. She, along with countless others, have to have come up with a story of how they are not enough, how they need something, be it food, alcohol, sex, something or someone to validate their intrinsic value – and when that does not occur what comes up is an unhealthy body, relationships gone wrong, ill-communication between one another because of the story that has been made up.

It has just occurred to me that when one is in denial or disassociated from the fact that it is all just a story, that you are magnificent of yourself, then the progression continues to perpetuate itself in various forms and you and yourself are ill-at-ease because of the creation that you are. You are totally disassociated from that.

Chapter Three

The Journey of Self-Discovery

The stories that we are telling ourselves!! — We treat each other as a result of the stories we are telling ourselves, about ourselves. Then that stuff just moves on down and relationships always, in my opinion, are indicative of the story you are telling yourself about yourself. So when you are telling yourself a story about you, can you imagine what you are doing – what I am doing to my fellowman? It behooves us – it behooves me, if I am going to write a story, to know it's alright. I can always begin again. You can always rewrite that story. If the story in your head is contaminated, if it's filled with thinking that does not serve you, does not serve this beautiful Planet, then you know unequivocally, rewrite your story; rewrite your story because energy flows wherever your attention goes and you might just want to rewrite your story that you've concocted, your story that is not serving you or anyone else.

Knowing that where my attention goes, energy flows, that is an awe of life. Is there any wonder that this Planet that we inhabit is the way it is? Our lack of not knowing that thought, that thinking is so crucial to what shows up for me, that what shows up for the Planet. We are powerful beings and don't have a clue of the power that embodies us. We can change the course of this Planet by thinking loving thoughts; by thinking healthy thoughts; thinking wealthy thoughts and then moving, as a result of our thinking, to action – action of those good, positive thoughts.

Most of my readers – some of my readers know that I frequent the social medium, Facebook and it is amazing the information that people put on Facebook. However, what I got is – we get back to the story!! – whatever storyline you have created, the words that you utter are a result of whatever storyline is going on. I don't know any other way to impact the masses except through this book and hopefully, countless readers are reading this book — that you and I are so powerful; that my very story results from my thinking; and so because I now know that, yes, you guessed it! I am going to be ever mindful of the stories I choose to concoct. And my mental health is flourishing now because now I know with whomever – family, associates – whomever I come in contact with, however they respond to me is directly a result of years of stories that people have concocted. That mountain of concocting shows up and it's doing what it is doing.

One of the ways that I know that thought is so powerful and that we totally – totally!! – act out of our thoughts is this:

About a week ago, I decided that I was going to walk 3 miles, 3 or 4 times a week. I first thought it; made the decision to act on that thought. It is June 11th and this morning, I acted on that thought. I walked 3, plus miles because it all began with a thought that I was totally cognizant of – WOW!!

I just put on Facebook a few minutes ago, a "Status" — that's what we call it, a "Status", that says "I am not surprised that you do not support me; I am not surprised that I do not get "Congrats" from you. What I get is, you are not there for yourself. WOW!! Of course, it is a story that I made up. But I also began to wonder: How many people have I made up stories about and these people are victims of possibly being sexually abused, physically abused, mentally abused and then I wonder in my grandiose story why people are not there for me. They don't know how!

And as I get it, that compassion for another fellow pilgrim on the Planet is so crème de la crème. It's the God way. It's the God-way because not knowing where a person has been or where he/she is, I don't get to sit in condemnation/ judgment (they both probably mean the same); I don't get to sit in condemnation when I don't know from whence a fellow pilgrim, a fellow journeyman has come. WOW! Talk about revelation!!

A lot of things I have concluded, that I'm thinking about other people and their behaviors, as I'm sitting here writing. It just came to me that this enlightenment that is occurring, it's occurring as a result of my own enlightenment. It's not about somebody else; it's about my being open to growing. It's about my being open to be transparent. And that is my goal – to always be transparent with myself because I am always transparent to God. But it is only until I am willing to be transparent to myself that I then will be wholeheartedly transparent to you. WOW!! And while I think that it is good to write stories about research that you have done, I believe it is crucial to, at first become brutally, if you will, transparent with yourself because then I am not being a façade and I don't know myself. Consequently, you don't know me because in my story, in my fear, I don't want you to know me. WOW!!

The Story

A couple of days ago, I was speaking to a very, very good friend of mine and we were talking about a time to depart for a [venue]. I began to share with my friend how I was deriving the time of departure. As I was talking to my friend, my friend interrupted and said, "We're not talking about that!" And I heard that. I got that. So I did not continue with that frame of conversing. Well, my friend called me back and made a startling statement. My friend said, "Do you think that is your brother's problem as well — that your brother does a lot of thinking and talks about a lot of things going on in his head?"

When my friend said, "We're not talking about that" – what I got is at that juncture my friend had no care to listen to what I was saying, to what I was sharing. I know that my friend spoke out of his storyline. And I stopped!! — at that juncture of sharing how I was coming up with a time frame for the venue.

The Downloading of Files into the Human Psyche

My friend then called me back and said, "Do you think that is what's going on with your brother, that your brother is having more conversation, or using more words than that is needed? Do you think that's what's wrong with him?" And I was startled at first. I called my friend back and said, "Low blow! Low blow!" What I got at that same time, my friend made up a story in his head and was treating me accordingly.

So as I am on this "journey" of discovery of stories that we make up, I am choosing to ever remain compassionate, although I am continuing to observe. Oh my! What a wonderful discovery!

And then I think of, as I said earlier in the book, of the decades that I and all of us, I am believing, have conjured up stories rather than getting to know the truth of any matter. I am thinking of a healthier Planet. I am thinking of authentic relationships.

You know – a friend of mine was getting ready to go and have carpal tunnel surgery (and of course here I go with my stories). (I chuckle at this moment.) What kind of toxic — toxic thinking!! — has been going on that has travelled down to my friend's wrist? The medical profession, if you will, has given it a name, Carpal Tunnel Syndrome, and what's really going on is a massive, massive negative sick thinking that has "tunneled" itself at our wrist and now our wrist is giving us untold anguish. Rather than deal with the facts, to go inside yourself and look at the very fact that it's my thinking that has caused this, I need to rewrite the stories that are going on in my head.

Chapter Four

A Storybook Life

*L*et me stop right here and share with you. There's a story always going on – always going on in your head. You are the author! So being the author, you might not be able to retract but you can always begin a new story; a new storyline that can eradicate the poison that's flowing in your body, that you are choosing to not acknowledge. By choosing to not acknowledge it, **THE BEAT GOES ON!!**

Watch this. Let's do a "for instance". You go to the doctor. The doctor cuts out, or opens up whatever is causing the carpal tunnel "stuff" and then even though that's done, "it" comes back! Or "it" comes back because you have not taken care of the mental toxicity that's running rampant in your body. You think it's something that surgery can fix. It all started in your head. Your body is sick! – because of a head problem.

Would you at least look at that? — that all of illness may truly be a result of head issues — head issues that may be quite simple to fix, to change and we have allowed ourselves to be bombarded with, "WE'LL CUT IT OUT, AND IT'LL BE OKAY." Not being a medical practitioner (and that's my disclaimer right here); if it's a head issue and it's affected your body, I am thinking at this juncture, cutting it out can't fix it because it all began with your thought life. WOW!!

Thinking here now that based on how I was reared, let me tell you; let me share with you some stories that I have made up and tried to make them applicable to other people. WOW. One story I made up in my own head was, you say "Hello" to people. You just speak to people. That was one story.

Another story is, I like you as a person, so it's only natural that you like me as a person. NOT!! NOT!! NOT!! I also made the story up in my mind that because I treat you right based on karma, you are going to do the same for me. I got that. That's another story.

Proceeding further with another story — I know how I will treat you on any given day based on the fact that my life typifies the love of God in my heart. So I am thinking that in my head that is how you are with me. I had no idea that there are fakes out there who will pretend and their heart is far from it (The Golden Rule). Just a real awakening for me of how the stories go on and on. What I have concluded in my own mind is as I am re-writing my stories, life is good for me.

Another wallop of a story that I am telling myself of that story as I am writing this book, is that based on how I talk to you and how you respond to me has something to do with my identity. And what I have gotten from that story that is a myth – totally a myth!! — how you talk to me is the story that you have in your head about me and it has no identifying marks as to who and what my value is. That is potent — potent !!

Based on my observation of people and stories they make up, I've observed that based on their stories they will **THROW YOU UNDER THE BUS**!! at a heartbeat! That is why it is so crucial, if you will, that you be aware as you are aware —know that as you write your story, as I write my stories, there is some good in the world; there are good people in the world and there are people who are writing stories because they themselves perceive that they have no value. They will and do treat you accordingly.

One of the things that has come to my mind, too, is when it comes to hoarding that hoarding, as I am coming to "revisit" this thing, is a result of people internally not feeling good enough. Therefore, they collect things upon things. Somehow they have made the story up that the things that they think they are collecting are going to give them identity, give them value. It's all an internal matter, created by made up stories. When the internal self is disturbed, its outward manifestation will be the countless, countless actions that are occurring. They do not have a purposeful vision of their life story, that they are truly beautiful people.

Seeing people as beautiful, beautiful souls is a magnanimous thing. They are personalities that the stories in their own heads have created. It is something that they must work at it, seeing themselves first and foremost as a beautiful soul. They are responsible for the personality that they continue to create or re-invent based on the stories that they themselves continue to concoct.

Have you ever concocted a story about you — that you matter and you've put this self-evaluation on the backburner?? That you are not first and foremost, that the greatest gift you can give this Planet is to love God firstly, to love yourself dearly and your neighbor will follow suit??!! WOW!!

Chapter Five

Living Life in a Capsule

The disassociation – what in your story do you disassociate the importance of a human life? Just had an interesting series of events occur this evening. My brother is in need of going to the hospital because of an infection in his arm. To my amazement, his immediate family members have their own agendas, and their agendas do not include taking care of the brother that needs hospital care urgently. The story that people are telling themselves is: "I've got this to do; let Joanne do it." What they don't know is, the story that I am telling myself — FAMILY FIRST!!

Yes, it's summer vacation from school for the children and I've been out of school for a week. This weekend is my granddaughter's graduation; my granddaughter's celebration party. However, it is amazing that people are choosing a "shade tree", if you will, for me to sit under. I will rise to the occasion because my brother, Joe, is most important at this juncture. No doubts about it!! But I'm putting it out there. The story that every one else seems to be telling: "I have to do this," or "I have to do that." And most jobs, as I know it, when you speak up and say you have a family emergency — I don't know of jobs that won't give you space for that. So it sounds to me like there's a story being told by individuals and it may be a fear factor; nonetheless, the story is being told.

But because I get it – God Almighty has given me all things that pertaineth to life and godliness. *(2nd **Peter 1:3**)*. I will transport my brother to the hospital in the morning. I will be prepared to valet park. And a human life is more important than any job, any waiting on the appliance man. I hear in everyone's story – "Let someone else do it." WOW!!

You know, it's blowing my mind, but it shouldn't, because what has been true for a gazillion years, you care about others the way you feel about you. And what you feel about you and your importance is "nil". Then it should not be a surprise when you feel the same about your family.

As I look at this issue, this happening, if you will, I have decided in my story, Man!! — I don't want these people on my team! Because on my team, I show up for people and I definitely want people on my team who will show up for me.

"Mister and Mz. Persnickety "– yes, you heard correctly — Persnickety!! — have obviously fallen into the abyss and in the abyss, insanity is running rampant. Insanity is running rampant even though you walk; you see; you talk; you do. Ignorant persnicketyness is at the summit of your beingness. And as I on a daily observance get the insanity, get the walking around in circles, clueless of your [own] persnicketyness ; and my story is: "Stay aware, Joanne; stay cognizant of the environment and tell a different story. Live a different story." That will be my contribution to this Planet.

Oftentimes it becomes so easy to go along to get along; to be a people-pleaser, because "they will like me if I don't rock the boat;" if I tell myself the same story that they themselves continue to tell. I get the vast opportunity to tell – and I am – a different story. WOW!! — WOW!!

I awakened this morning with a multiplicity of thanksgiving in my heart. I awakened this morning so thrilled to be alive; so thrilled to be sitting on my deck, drinking coffee and being aware – being aware, watching the birds play, watching the birds sing. I don't know how much of a brain a bird has, but I don't see the birds telling stories or acting out stories (although they might be). What I do see is the birds behaving joyfully – joyfully at their existence and we get up as human beings oftentimes with a preset agenda.

Smiles don't phase us because the agenda is paramount. The agenda is, "I've got to get up and I've got to make it happen!" Well, let me share with you, my readers, this morning. As I said, I get to tell myself the story: "Just be still! Just sit, basking in all of the elation, but I'm joyous to be in this space, this time, with nothing but sheer love." My wish is all goodness, all love for the whole Planet.

My story right now?? – I'm aware of it, and this is what I would suggest to you, my loves, my readers: **Take time to be aware of the story that you concoct.** I want to suggest that the very story that you concoct has to do with your well being. If your well being is challenged, (I want to put it out there), your well being is challenged based on the story that you very well may be unaware of. The story I'm telling myself is to "ENJOY LIFE!"

I want to regress a little bit or backtrack. Yesterday, I had some Johnny Taylor music on, playing and just decided to enjoy and to dance and to smile and see the story that may have been told me; the stories as Johnny Taylor was doing his thing. Laugh! Enjoy life! And the other story I'm telling myself is, "Stop being so serious; smile!" The body loves it. The body loves it. (Repeat).

Just called a friend of mine; she will remain anonymous. I'm just going to call her "V". As we started to talk this morning, I said, "An awesome inspiring day to you." And she started to telling me that she still has this trouble with her arm. She said, "You didn't know I broke my arm about a year ago." And she went on to say that it's not working well. She's got arthritis in her neck and in her back, and she just had a horrific story going on. She went on "to claim" that age, in her story, is a derivative of what's going on with her. The she concluded: "Well; you know that I've got to complain."

Well now!! She woke up with that story in regard to her arm. I asked her, "Are you doing therapy?" She said: "Yes, but something has delayed the therapy." So she is walking around with her story.

What I'm getting about all stories is there is nothing that another human being can do with someone else's story. What you can do and what I am doing is, I am being aware of that; that is her story. She is giving that story energy. So the energy that she is projecting into that story will reap time and time again. Somebody has said that "Karma is a mother**@@!!" WOW!! So I'm listening — and I'm listening to her this Saturday morning and I'm thinking, "Oh my!!" But this is her story.

The other thing I'm getting is I need not make judgments; I need not make condemnation because to her, that's life; to her, that's real. Being real in her story, I don't get to discredit her story. If she is choosing to become disassociated with all the beauty in life and take ownership of the story of her lack-luster of life – it is what it is!!

And so as she and I concluded our conversation, I got that; that's her story. I didn't call for that, but whenever I make a phone call, I must take responsibility that no one put a gun to my head and made me make that phone call. What I can do, as soon as space presents, when that story has energy that is debilitating – as soon as I can—you know the deal: I've got to get off the phone!! Much love.

Chapter Six

Word Power: Self-Evolving

A great power walk this morning, I had!! What stories do you tell yourself when you're doing your workout? This morning it occurred to me as I took my laps around the track, as I was doing my workout – no one can walk for me. No one can put in the energy to perfect my health, my body for me. It is something that I will have to do to get results.

In his consistent use of the ever-wise, Thomas Jefferson, Bob Foley said**, *"In order to get something you do not have, you've got to be willing to do something you've never done."*** So there's no osmosis. There's no story you can tell yourself to get the desired results from walking. My suggestion is: You want good health; you want to feel good?? – then you've got to put it out there. Pump those arms; walk those 12 laps or more around the track and feel good. Do those affirmations – affirmations add energy, health to the bone, to the whole body. You are deserving of it. Tell yourself some good stories out on that track. Good stories!

My "self"-inventory – really looking into my incessant story making up: When I am looking at me and the stories that I've made up, all of the stories have been just that – no real value, no truth to them.

I was thinking about George Senior. As I look at George and I see his **beautiful, beautiful soul** – What an amazing creation when I look at his soul! He is so giving; he is so loving. When I make the stories up that have to do with the earth-suit of clothing that he is wearing and which is just right for him – when I look at his personality, I begin to distort the real beautiful soul that George inhabits. At this juncture, I just want to say, "Thank you, God! Thank you for the connection. Thank you for letting me come to know such a beautiful, beautiful soul." A **beautiful soul** that is daily working. I see him working at no longer being judgmental of mankind and I have learned so much because I am allowing myself to learn. I'm allowing myself to admit: You made up a lot of stories and the stories are causing me to grow when I am being open and realizing – "Boy! Lots of stories there." In actuality, what a good human being; what a good soul ! I am ever thankful to continue to sojourn with this beautiful soul on Planet Earth.

It has come to my attention that our very posture is indicative of how we view ourselves. How do you view yourself, pitiful or powerful? What story are you harboring about you that you walk around, drooping shoulders, slumped body? It must be a hideous story you are telling yourself about you. Your health has a story about you as well. Are you loving, healthy, wealthy and strong? Maybe it's time to come face to face about how God made you.

I HEARD – some folks saying a while back — "God did not create you to be necessarily healthy, but He did create you to be spiritually sound." I happen to think they go hand in hand. If you are truly spiritually sound, then the way you care for your body will be a gigantic indicator of that as well — how you glorify God in your body.

I am also of the opinion that we put things on God that are foreign to Him. **We indict God!!** in things that we've concocted and the gambit runs rampant.

I recently had a co-ed family summit scheduled for June 2012. I started to posting it on Facebook in April 2012, giving each household enough time to move things around to attend, should they desire. I requested that each family member bring a fruit tray. I would make ready the house, provide spa water and express coffee. I bought fresh flowers, yellow carnations to be exact, put tuber roses in a vase to greet guests, and guess what happened? Fourteen guests came of those who RSVP'ed. Although I wanted to feel a little devastated, I had to take responsibility for the story I made up in April and family members were not fitting the storyline that I concluded. What I had to conclude was "LIFE IS LIFE!!" – and it shows up in a multi-faceted way. People have lives and it shows up for them in various ways. Those that attended, it showed up for them the way it showed up. What I trust is that at that family summit, that those who attended got their necessary lessons in attending. I DID!! And what happens is, you move on.

Let me put it out there, "rat" now!! (R.A.T., in my Ebonics!!) Making up the story that people speak by the way of saying, "Good Morning," on a day to day basis when they see one another, or "Good Afternoon," etc. – it's good etiquette, sure. But it's a concoction of itself. For decades, I fostered that story. I fully embraced that mannerism is a great thing to embrace and I get joy from that mannerism. Most of the people I meet seem to enjoy that as well. It adds a spark to my well-being that,

that mannerism I am not ashamed to enjoy. I am exhilarated in being a participant in that.

"Thank You" is another story that I concocted — WOW!! When someone does something for me or gives me something, I say, "Thank You" and with exhilaration! I was reared that way and all the tea in China will not change that in me. I do not desire to be any other way in that regard.

My son who lives with me works two jobs. I decided on one particular day to cook for him, to have a meal ready for him, at his desire. So I seasoned some chicken breasts, and browned it in some olive oil – very nicely browned and simmered it for ever how long. In addition, I added some broccoli florets (10 minutes) and set it aside to bask in its seasoning and brown rice on the side. I felt really good having done that. He came in and fixed it "to go" for lunch for work and never said, "Thank you". I was floored! However, because of the story again that I concocted of how it was supposed to go, not that it was not appreciated – he just never said, "Thank you". That was my feeling — transferring my rearing to my son. Thus the world at large, it goes on.

Self expression is a privilege and a right. Judging my son on the basis of my self expression and not accepting his non-expression is not quite right. Man! When the student is ready, the teacher shows up everywhere! LOL (laughing out loud). My point in sharing this is the grief, the feeling, the disgruntleness on the heels of self-inflicted laws, making those laws for others is a huge injustice to God and to me and to others. Who said that that person is an ingrate person? Where do I – where do you get to legislate another's intentions solely on your own (my own) pre-conceived biases?

Chapter Seven

The Life of Domestication

Domestication is another huge set of rules that we live out of. Domestication is a hard taskmaster. We are on "auto"-domestication. You know what domestication is. We have been "tamed", "trained", "disciplined", "schooled" "house-trained", "subjugated"!! You've heard of a domesticated animal, or someone's domestication is someone that has been groomed on a certain behavior type of lifestyle. That is why I say that domestication is a hard taskmaster. How we view others; what we think others mean, at any given moment — we get ourselves in so much havoc because of our previous domestication – she meant that or he meant that; no utterance from him or from her as to what they really meant. Based on previous domestication, previous perception is where I believe my peace is distorted and the perception and the recipient both are distorted.

Yes; domestication – when I say that we are on auto-pilot in domestication from infancy, you and I have been trained. We've learned certain behaviors and in the blink of an eye, you and I start living out of that domestication. If you're honest with yourself, as I am willing to be honest with myself, at this point — All of my life up to this point – that I have been willing to be aware of is domestication, where I am willing to surrender that. Yes!! — I don't give much thought out of what I do or what I say because living on auto-pilot, what I do, what I say, and even what I think arise out of my previous and yes, even my ongoing domestication — WOW!!

This previous domestication that I am believing — I am persuaded, is from perception, projection and I believe that my peace becomes distorted and it is **EATING MY LUNCH!!** This previous domestication has taken me through some illusions, and the process of awareness has to set; the process of awareness has to set in order for there to be an understanding of this domestication behavior. Acting out of the downloading of the mental, the physical and yes, even the spiritual abuse have to and will evoke havoc. Seeing my worth; you seeing your worth — out of the downloading files!! The domestication that comes on, automatically.

The downloading comes about in so many facets. If you think that you are accidentally allowing yourself to be mentally, physically, and yes, spiritually abused, you need to think again. You have downloaded files about your worth and consequently have subjected yourself to heinous behaviors and they will evoke havoc. They can also cause you to go through something that is called "desensitization" and when it gets onboard, when you are told long enough that, "You don't matter"; when you're told that, "You're crazy"; when you're told long enough to, "Shut up!" — Is there any wonder that your emotions become callous? Low self-esteem sets in. All manner of evil is displayed. Living as an appendage to others can become a way of life. I believe that is co-dependent behavior that is alive and well.

CHAPTER EIGHT

The Brain: The Files in the Human Computer

Talking about downloading files!! The virus that is in the brain that causes this downloading in the first place — there has to be a willingness to analyze and come to terms with the fact that this **domestication,** the fact that this downloading has occurred in order for a clearing up of this heinous virus to take place.

Whether you agree or not, all actions are strong indicators that a trauma is influencing all actions. When I say "trauma", I mean "the forced action that consistently reeks havoc for you and those you come in contact with on a daily basis". Some people take it to be a natural phenomenon; a conscious or unconscious action, it matters not. The consequences are the same.

The Downloading of Files into the Human Psyche

One thing that has happened in my own life is that I was believing that I had a friend. And the downloaded files from my friend "resurrected" and because I was not acting according to my friend's downloaded files, the profile that "my friend" had so set in place for me, I again, Oh my God!! – I made a story up that my friend "was my friend". Today, I'm not sure that my friend is not my friend. What I do believe is and what I need to have compassion about is, although my friend may very well be my friend (and it sounds as though I'm continuing to regurgitate the same thing) that based on my friend's domestication allowing me to be who I am was not even on the table because of prior downloaded files. So the friendship becomes in jeopardy because there was this unspoken genre, if you will, that this is how I am to behave; this is how the profile has been set up and when you don't live out of that profile that has been set, then you're no longer acceptable as a friend. O.M.G.!!

The only way to de-program the downloading that has haunted all of us for decades is to be willing to be open and to do the necessary work to become whole as I believe was intended for the whole Planet. Relaxing into your innate, God-given self and begin to live the abundant life; accept the fact that we have erred on the side of ignorance.

I went on a journey in the 1900s, a journey of running from myself, inflicting downloads after downloads, thinking that I was not safe – all of this was fearful downloads, self- inflicted. I installed and made them a reality. Oh, the struggle to be free as I was created to be !!

The mind incessantly engaging in thought that I was in fact in danger – the danger that I was exposed to was the danger of not getting that I am always safe. I am in a space of being provided for by Almighty God. I am always safe. Now there will be those of you who are reading this book that will beg to differ and the right you have to believe that, to differ . What I finally am getting is that **God did not create me and then not provide safety for me.** As I choose, (and He lets me choose) — as I choose to trust that safety. WOW!!

What downloaded file are you living out of that you don't question the medical profession when it comes to your own health? The professionals, if they will, whether or not they are in professional integrity or not – are they in fact playing God, deciding that if one is of age and by age, I mean in their 80's — Does the medical profession then make a decision and you trust that decision? The decision is that they have lived a long life, so let's just make them comfortable at this juncture in their lives. Seriously ??!! Our lives are valuable; we matter!

Although there are those who take it ever so lightly, who gets to place value on our lives unless we give them the permission? When we step into a medical professional's office, it is then that the permission has been granted most of the time to do whatever they deem is the right thing to do.

Chapter Nine

Revisiting Past Downloads

I chose most recently to patronize a colleague whom I decided in time past not to any longer patronize that colleague. Again, when I decided to patronize that colleague **again,** who had not given me change [due to me] **previously** for a product, I stepped right into the fire **again**, and patronized that colleague **again**. The product cost was $3.99; I gave the colleague $5.00 and the colleague acted as though I was not due change. What I got from that was, I needed, and I did, take responsibility that, that I gave her permission **to repeat** that same behavior toward me and this time I got the lesson. She treated me as though, based on my downloaded file, based on my perception that she had value and integrity. My expectation was, "Give me the change due to me!"

My new "reveal" is that when you have any dealings with a human being, "Be prepared not to make that same mistake!" So as I say that when you are dealing with any human being, be prepared; be prepared. Do not mistake me; the world is a beautiful place. I love it; I love the inhabitants. Now, the inhabitants can be a different story. Again— **AWARENESS IS KEY**. Yes –AWARENESS is a huge deal, because you cannot begin to deal with yourself if you're clueless to the need to implement self-improvement.

I heard recently, "You can lead a human being to knowledge, but **YOU CANNOT MAKE THEM THINK**!" How profound is that! Another astronomical gem.

To embrace your need to grow, say it, on a recorder, if you need to! I remain acutely aware of the need to grow, for maximum mental, spiritual, and physical growth, I could go on and on as I continue to evolve. The Planet will become an ever better place to inhabit — an awakening indeed. I have shared what I have shared because to do so or not to do so would be for me to die.

For me not to share what I am sharing with you as I become more enlightened about this myself, would be to experience an untimely spiritual death. How many of us die with our music still inside of us? The spark, the splendor is just gone! How tragic! So, where do we go from here? What is our recourse? To know our own intrinsic value, that we are undisputedly fabulous creations of God, meant to do outrageously, marvelous things to impact the world in a potent, prolific, profound way, that will even cause [this] writer, yes, me, to be infectious, to rise in my own vibrations. My health, my wealth will escalate, relaxing into "just being"! — which can be a beautiful thing.

As with my previous book, **Your Thought Life**, my goal, my one goal is to inspire, to motivate, to share for the greater good of the Planet. Someone has said, ***"The gift you give to others is a gift that you give to yourself."*** Sometimes we're in the fast lane of life and on a destructive path, blindly foraging ahead. What a self-destructive motif – the download is activated!

Our belief system is a huge part of who we are. Our self-image — we live out of that. Listen to how we talk. Is it gloom and doom? Is it joy, love and peace — all of the [fruit] of the Spirit (**Galatians 5:22-23),** we are free to live out of? Or does your belief system encompass only you? Your life is worth serious consideration. Don't be afraid to look at you and your behavior. How you behave is who you have chosen to become.

Your belief system; really look at that. Pause here to really look at it. When you look at me, when I look at you, we are our chosen belief system. The downloaded data — mentally, physically and spiritually — so powerful because thoughts are real. Thoughts are a real force, transferrable and yes, we put stuff into the world based on how we have downloaded our belief system that we have set up.

Who have you chosen to give your power to? Who in your life has [affected] you to the point that they have convinced you that when you give your power to somebody else under the guise of being a good person; under the guise of being a Christian; under the guise of being humble — who have you given your power away to?

As I am writing this part of this book, I am feeling somewhat infuriated; I am feeling a little animosity here because as I am thinking this about others, I have, year after year, under the guise of my being a good mother; under the guise of my being a good mother-in-law; under the guise of my being even a Christian!! — And what I have done? I have given my power to other individuals and in the process, I have demeaned myself. You guessed it !! That is part of that unconscious awareness of that downloaded file. And all I have to do is "click" that file.

I can either edit that file or delete that file, especially now that I have become acutely aware that this file does not serve me.

There will be those that will strive with all of the fiber of their being to convince you that you got it wrong, and that will be part of that manipulating that has been going on for years and years. It is time to step up! to stand up! – in my God-given power to understand with your God-given power, you can be all that you can be as a fellow- journeyman, a fellow-journeywoman. That's my gift; that's your gift from God. And because others do not understand their God-given power and are out to "slurp" your power, let them know it is not for sale; IT IS NOT FOR SALE!

You have a gift; stand up for that gift. God did not create you to let somebody else feel good at your expense. We've all been given that gift; that gift to live "victorious"; that gift to live "tenacious"; that gift to live triumphantly! We've all been given "the gift". Don't give yours to somebody else.

Actually, today, August 23, 2012, I am not making up stories today. What a joy! I'm staying in the zone today; I'm staying in the moment. I am sure that [removable] of these made-up stories is possible, upon awareness and the willingness to look at the evidence that downloading files is causing my life, your life, to run amuck.

CHAPTER TEN

The Power of Affirmations on Downloaded Files

As I was thinking about how in the world can so many downloaded files that have contaminated our existence, how can that begin to change? Well, it has been said that it takes 21 days to change a habit. My suggestion is, 21days of your choosing affirmations that would replace the acting out of downloaded files. My suggestions [is] possibly an affirmation that says, "Today, I live in the moment; **TODAY!!** I live in the moment." Today, I will not allow downloaded files to run my life in a destructive way. I am suggesting that repeating that on a daily basis when you recognize that you are living out of that conglomerate of downloaded files — I am suggesting that for 21 days, when awareness comes that you are living out of that, then go and re-direct yourself by doing affirmations

The Downloading of Files into the Human Psyche

until that moment of acting out of that downloaded file system in your head has ceased. We've got to start somewhere! And this is "my" suggestion; a great starting place. It may take some people longer than 21 days. Let's face it. The downloaded files, they exist; they exist.

Chapter Eleven

HodgePodge Ethics: Turning the Corner

*B*ecome a fly on the wall with me, if you will and let's look at a download:

A married couple has beautiful children. Because of one of the spouse's download, the other spouse became a dictator in the family. The spouse that became a dictator in the family perceived from their own previous download that their children were not to be reprimanded. The other spouse (and I'll call "the other non-aggressive spouse") a non-factor spouse because that's what this other spouse became – TRIED!! with all of their might to create some respect, some parameters for those children and the dictator spouse continued to check, if you will, check the non-factor spouse — to check that spouse over and over in the presence of the children,

The Downloading of Files into the Human Psyche

again until the children began to treat the non-factor spouse as non-factor.

The dictator spouse [was adamant about using their previous downloads] reproving the non-factor spouse in the presence of the children. As it was, the dictator spouse would call that non-factor spouse out in front of the children to berate, to demean!! And what do you know??!! The dictator spouse created a group of children (and I observed this myself, from port to port to port) — I observed these children treat the non-factor parent with disdain. I observed those children look at that non-factor spouse as though [to say], "How dare you check me!"

I have observed first hand those children talk to the non-factor spouse in a very non-factor way. If you at all can see the picture now: these children are teenagers now all except for one and they literally – LITERALLY!! — treat that non-factor parent as has been instructed by example from that dictator parent. WOW!!

So, somehow that non-factor parent with their learned behavior, their belief system, continued to live out that learned behavior and that dictator spouse grew enormous, astronomical in their behavior and the spouse that had one goal, one aim and that is to bring those children up in a society where respect is paramount. But that spouse, that dictator spouse reigns supremely.

And here goes my downloaded file. When you feed the beast, the beast can do nothing but grow, and grow, and grow, and grow! It is my observation, at this point, that the spouse that was treated as non-factor doesn't even know who they are at this point. They have, in my observation, caved in to that massive dictator of a spouse. Talk about downloading files!! Forgetting your origin!! — God has never created one individual to be superior to another. And when you feed that energy, when you feed that vibration, it can only grow out of control. O my goodness!!

What I want to say at this juncture is that the non-factor spouse is responsible to become aware; aware of what they have allowed and the dictator of a spouse is equally responsible to look at that massive, grotesque behavior of the dictator and to create a loving file —- a life to where they matter and they know it and all others are treated accordingly.

In my opinion, Hitler has nothing on this dictator spouse because as the dictator spouse has infected those children, if those children do not or choose not to become aware of their lethal behavior, they will go out [into a world] and they will create others as themselves.

Hitler??!! WOW! – What an example! And then, I can't blame Hitler. I am responsible; you are responsible for all that has happened to you in your life. O, my goodness!

So, what I want to say about God at this point: God has given all of us all things that pertaineth to life and godliness. (*2nd Peter 1:3*) So as the picture that I have just painted for you – there are no victims here. There are only those that have chosen to become blindsided by another's negative, defiled energy.

Chapter Twelve

Developing a File of Safe Thinking

Some of you may be wondering or saying as you are reading this particular page – How in the world, now that I get it, that my downloads are processed gazillion times after gazillion times; who then can eradicate the multiplicity of downloads? I have great news for you; I have great news. Just as you hit a delete button on a computer, you can hit the delete button on the hard drive of your brain. It may be that for you this is a lifestyle change. It may be that you do this for the rest of your life, but it is worth it.

When you are aware that the multiplicity of contaminated, infectious files live inside of your brain, you get to choose. Everyday you choose — downloaded files; contaminated. Let it go! Replace it with an affirmation. I'm thinking of one right now and that is: "I AM STRONG!! I AM STRONG!! I AM STRONG!!" And believe that. As you listen to that affirmation, that I AM

STRONG, and I have confidence, I have confidence; believe in yourself. No, you're not mechanical, but you are a human being with a vast intelligence. So, let's get to it; let's get to it.

Start to hit that delete button on the hard drive of your brain; start to say to yourself, "I can do all things through Christ who strengtheneth me." (***Philippians 4:13***) And I will begin right now.

What's up??!! Downloaded file!!?? Contaminated file coming through!! "I can do all things through Christ who gives me the strength." I no longer choose that downloaded file. And you do that moment by moment on a daily basis, and I promise you that you are going to experience a freedom as never before. Believe that you can delete; you can do a clean sweep, a clean sweep of that hard drive on your brain and make it new.

One writer summed it up as this de-contamination process:

" . . . Whatsoever things are true;

Whatsoever things are honest;

Whatsoever things are just;

Whatsoever things are pure;

Whatsoever things are lovely;

Whatsoever things are of good report;

…[THINK]onthesethings." ***(Philippians 4:8)***

Chapter Thirteen

Thinking Outside "The Box"

Wondering why your life has gone amuck: It has gone amuck because you do not possibly get it that God in his infinite wisdom has given us all a brain to think. However, we have listened incessantly to others' thinking, and our own thinking most of the time has become "nil". We have downloaded a file because someone else aggressively has spoken and we put our own thinking on the back burner and decided that according to the override, if you will, of the file of somebody else's thinking, we have made that thinking paramount. So we are limping into life not knowing why we are limping into life because we have allowed a technology override, if you will, of our thinking and preferred someone else's thinking to our own thinking. WOW!!

I am just reminding myself of the fact that I recently made a decision that I did not want a negative energy in the sphere of my ambiance, my environment and because I made that decision, there are those who have risen up to say even that I myself said what I didn't say, because they have become mighty in their own thinking and, therefore, want to make what I think, "nil". How disrespectful of your own self that your thinking does not matter, that you now want to make my thinking of no consequence! I get to decide whether or not I want negative energy or positive energy in the sphere of my "beingness".

Because of my incessant struggle, WOW!! — of allowing others' thinking to be paramount, it has become most challenging for me at this era of my life to know that my thinking matters. One does not have to agree with my thinking, but, HOW DARE YOU!! — How dare you to try to make my thoughts of no consequence and your thoughts are the those of the hour! God has made all of us important. God has said, "You treat others the way you want to be treated." If you do not want me to treat you of no consequence, then you treat me the same, that my thinking has value. I also get it, however, that when you have been, or have allowed yourself to be treated, and to be "overrided", that your thinking matters — now you want to bring that to the table and be insistent, insisting that my thinking doesn't matter. Come on! Come on now!! Come on now! WOW!

CHAPTER FOURTEEN
Integrative Thinking

I am filled with gratitude, filled with gratitude! – that God has allowed this awareness in me. I get to share this with you, my readers, that the downloaded files that you consciously or unconsciously downloaded – I get to share with you that you can delete those files and "install" a new hardware on your brain. Okay, Joanne; so hardware on my brain; what does that look like? WOW! I'm so glad you asked.

First of all, the new hard drive of your brain looks like this. There is a Creator who has created us all with value. Put that on the hard drive of your brain – that you have value and those files that you installed [previously], they're no longer pertinent. You get it now, that you do have value and know on this new hard drive that there are those who are still living out of that previous download. They think that they are on the Planet to orchestrate your life and most of the time that demonic download wants to be insistent that, "You don't know how to think! I'm going to tell you how to think!" NOT!!

I have value; you have value. I may not think like you. You may not think like I think, but as long as your thinking is God-centered, your thinking is so on point on the new hardware. How epic is that? No one gets to look at you in your face, or NOT!! — and sublimally try to insert themselves as, **"YOU DON'T KNOW HOW TO THINK! I'M THINKING FOR YOU. SO, LISTEN UP!"** That is what has happened to most of us. And so something is wrong. At this point, we may go to drugs of all kind because we don't get it, that what someone else has installed in your brain, you can delete that and set yourself on a course of all good.

Chapter Fifteen

A Positive, Projected Future

This book would be incomplete if I did not stress the fact that taking total responsibility for the files that have been downloaded into the human psyche is and can be deleted no matter how encrypted the file may be – be it your health physically; be it mentally; be it spiritually. The negative download can be deleted. The hard drive of your brain is so intricate and it has been so designed that you can create a new pathway in the brain, a new paradigm, if you will, to energize a new way of thinking. You are not a victim unless it is of your own choosing. If you are choosing the route of victimization, then the consequences as well are yours.

You and I have been created to maximize our stay here on this Planet, to impact others. There is nothing enlightening about your choosing to "play small". In fact, if I would be a bit crass here, no one cares! But when you, in your awareness, look at your indoctrination, you would gasp: "Hey, look! An encrypted file here I've downloaded and it is not serving me." There is a way out – a way out to live that victorious life that others may see, that others may even choose to stand up. Delete that encrypted file and live! Live! Live!

If you choose to get what I am striving to share with you in this book, by way of a personal agenda, by way a personal looking at self, then I salute you. If you do not choose, I salute you. What I know is that self-development has to begin by looking at a need to do differently. There is a mold that has been cast, a "die" that has been cast and I can,(you can) choose to cast a new "dye" (that's D-Y-E), a new "dye" to living a different way.

But what I got here is there has to be a looking at and seeing the need for change. If I am in denial (and you are in denial), there will be no looking at self in view of changing. Changing is a healthy, a wise gift to self. I can this day be a prisoner of the past or a pioneer of the future, and blow this world to a new height because I am willing to be a pioneer rather than a prisoner of my future.

A Positive, Projected Future

You have heard me say "willing" or use the term "willing" often because I get it. I get it, that unless there is a willingness to look at and then to be a doer of what needs to happen, all of my efforts are useless, in vain.

I just put a "Status" on Facebook yesterday; this is July 5th, 2013. The "Status" was in the form of a question: Who told you that you were fat?? – that you were ugly?? — that you would never amount to anything?? — that you never do anything right?? — that you were stupid?? — that you were less than smart?? — Who told you and now you have plugged into what you have been told!! Who told you that lie?? And then you proceeded to download that file and you are now living out of that encrypted file, that lie!

Let's look at something, for example. Look at your health. How is your health today? Have you by chance been given a diagnosis and that diagnosis is a result of an encrypted file that you downloaded, that you are living out of, and your health is a derivative of that downloaded sick lie?

Spiritually – Do you wake up in the morning on a new high to live life, to give what has been given to you? How is that working for you?

And, mentally — No one is in charge of your mental download except you; no one. What are you choosing to think? Is it a result of your previous downloads? And you are acting as though that download has you hostage? Wait!! Maybe it does have you hostage, and shame on you!! – for valuing yourself so little.

Stand up! Look at the downloaded files. Look at the ones that are encrypted and know your intrinsic value is far more than you are living.

Chapter Sixteen

Conclusion

When I am open to freeing myself, freeing others is a given. Locking my energy up inside myself is like locking myself up, therefore, downloading of files that are deleterious to my well being, and to the Planet at large.

Learned behavior is to shut yourself off to others. Remaining open can be a catalyst to evolving and to the sensational creature that God created, rather than remaining stagnant and stunted, adhering to a vibration, a non-factor. What if I told you that because you are sitting does not necessarily mean that you are still. Stillness is a state of mind, body, and soul. True [still] is when the aforementioned are truly still – no incessant movement. All is harmonious. As an ancient prophet said, ". . . Their strength is to sit still." (*Isaiah 30:7*)

Works Cited

Foley, Bob. Thomas Jefferson Encyclopedia.

Galatians, chapter 5, verses 22-23. Holy Bible, King James Version. United States: Thomas Nelson Publishers, 1976.

Isaiah, chapter 30, verse 7. Holy Bible, King James Version. United States: Thomas Nelson Publishers, 1976.

Peter, Book II, chapter 1, verse 3. Holy Bible, King James Version. United States: Thomas Nelson Publishers, 1976.

Philippians, chapter 4, verses 8, 13. Holy Bible, King James Version. United States: Thomas Nelson Publishers, 1976.

Proverbs, chapter 23, verse 7. Holy Bible, King James Version. United States: Thomas Nelson Publishers, 1976.

www.ingramcontent.com/pod-product-compliance
Ingram Content Group UK Ltd.
Pitfield, Milton Keynes, MK11 3LW, UK
UKHW041956230426
12048UKWH00008B/368